LEO HOROSCOPE & ASTROLOGY 2025

Mystic Cat

Suite 41906, 3/2237 Gold Coast HWY

Mermaid Beach, Queensland, 4218

Australia

islandauthor@hotmail.com

Copyright © 2024 by Mystic Cat

Time set to Coordinated Universal Time Zone (UT±0)

All rights reserved. This book or any portion thereof may not be reproduced or used in any manner without the publisher's express written permission except for the use of brief quotations in a book review.

The information accessible from this book is for informational purposes only. None of the data should be regarded as a promise of benefits. It should not be considered a statutory warranty or a guarantee of results achievable.

Images are used under license from Fotosearch & Dreamstime.

Contents

January	16
February	24
March	32
April	40
May	48
June	56
July	64
August	72
September	80
October	88
November	96
December	104

Hello there, lovely readers! Let me explain why my horoscope books may give different readings for each zodiac sign. The sky is always bustling with astrological activity, and I want to focus on what's most important for each star sign.

Every zodiac sign is unique, and the planets up above affect them differently. When I create horoscopes, I pay extra attention to the most critical astrological events for a specific sign. Some days, there might be lots of stuff happening in the stars, but one thing stands out as the essential factor for a particular zodiac sign.

I also consider which planet rules a sign and its associated element. This in-depth consideration helps me tailor my interpretations to match a sign's characteristics.

Ultimately, my goal is to provide you with unique advice and insights that match the cosmic influences for your sign. By focusing on what makes each sign special, I hope to help you understand yourself better and navigate the energies around you. Embracing your sign's strengths and challenges is the key to making my horoscopes feel uniquely aligned for you.

Cosmic Blessings,

Sia Sands

LEO 2025
HOROSCOPE & ASTROLOGY

Four Weeks Per Month

Week 1 – Days 1 - 7

Week 2 – Days 8 - 14

Week 3 – Days 15 - 21

Week 4 – Days 22 – Month-end

LEO

Dates: July 23rd – August 22nd

Zodiac Symbol: Lion

Element: Fire

Planet: Sun

House: Fifth

Colors: Purple, gold

Leo is the fifth astrological sign in the zodiac and is associated with the Fire element. Individuals born under the Leo sign are known for their confidence, charisma, and creativity. Leo is vibrant, confident, and charismatic and tends to be lucky. The symbol of Leo, the lion, represents leadership, courage, and a strong sense of self.

Leo individuals exude natural magnetism and the ability to command attention. They often strongly desire to be in the spotlight and express themselves creatively. Ruled by the Sun, the center of our solar system, Leos have a radiant energy that draws people toward them and fills them with enthusiasm.

Leo is in the Fifth House of the zodiac, which is associated with creativity, self-expression, and enjoyment. This placement highlights Leo's need for self-expression and desire to engage in activities that bring joy and fulfillment.

The color gold is often associated with Leo due to its connections with warmth, success, and confidence. This color reflects the generous and radiant qualities of Leo individuals. It also reflects the royal and confident nature of Leo.

In summary, Leo represents confidence, creativity, and leadership. Those born under this sign tend to be passionate, expressive, and driven to make a positive impact. Their charismatic nature and ability to inspire others make them natural leaders and influencers in various aspects of life.

The Chinese Zodiac is a system that assigns an animal sign to each year in a 12-year cycle, and each animal is associated with certain personality traits and characteristics.

The Year of the Snake, in particular, holds special significance within Chinese culture and is rich in symbolism.

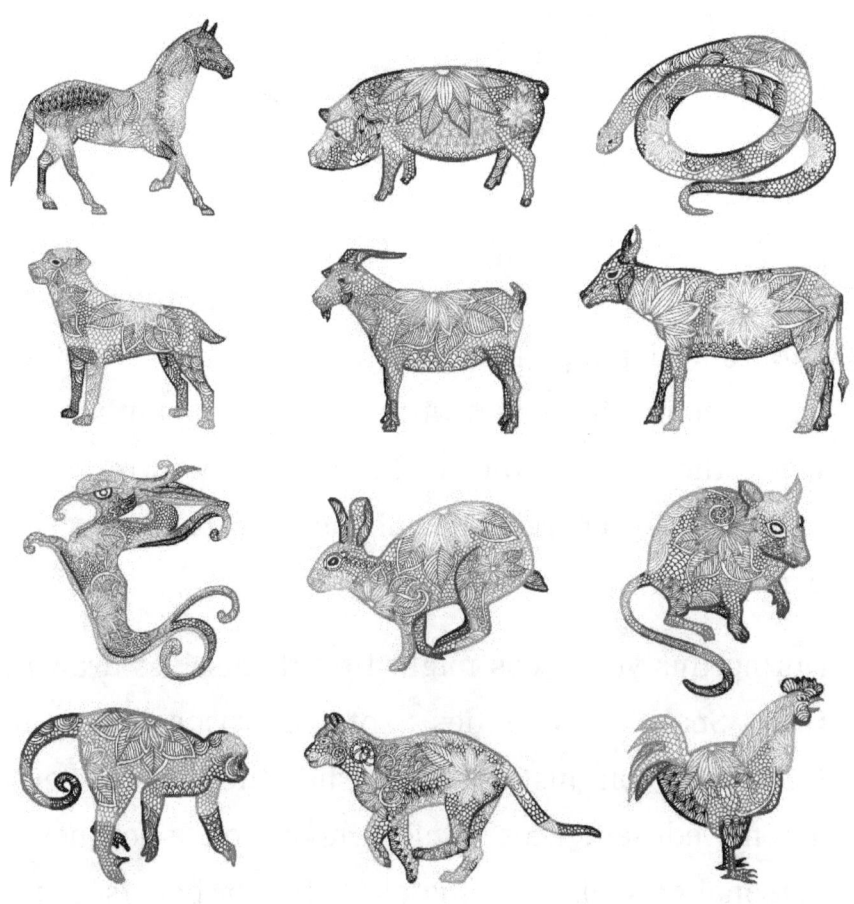

2025

The Chinese Year of the Snake

Leos are known for their charisma, confidence, and natural leadership qualities. They thrive in the spotlight and often inspire others with creativity and enthusiasm. When the Year of the Snake arrives, it introduces a unique set of energies to enhance and challenge Leo's personality.

During this year, Leos might find themselves drawn to the Snake's qualities of introspection and transformation. Just as snakes shed their skin to reveal a renewed self, Leos could embark on a journey of personal growth, shedding old habits or beliefs that no longer serve them.

The Year of the Snake encourages Leos to balance their natural self-assuredness with a more measured approach. It's a time for them to consider the long-term implications of their actions and decisions, much like the Snake's careful planning before striking.

Leos' natural magnetism and desire for recognition can resonate with the Snake's enigmatic charm. This year might inspire Leos to captivate others through a blend of confidence and depth, fostering connections that go beyond the surface.

The Year of the Snake could encourage Leos to explore their emotional depth in relationships. Just as snakes navigate their surroundings with keen perception, Leos might discover new layers within themselves and their loved ones, leading to more authentic and meaningful connections.

While Leos are known for their boldness, the Year of the Snake invites them to explore their inner selves. It doesn't mean diminishing their shine; it's about embracing personal growth and transformation while shining brightly in their unique way.

Ultimately, the Year of the Snake offers Leo an opportunity for self-discovery and external influence. By tapping into the Snake's symbolism of shedding the old and embracing the new, Leos can refine their approach to leadership, deepen their relationships, and continue to inspire others with a combination of charisma and depth.

LEO 2025
HOROSCOPE & ASTROLOGY

JANUARY WEEK ONE

The Moon's transition into Capricorn signifies a time of ambition and practicality. You feel the call to roll up your sleeves and tackle those long-term goals with determination and focus. Capricorn's energy encourages you to take a structured approach to your emotions, making it an excellent period for working on your professional life, setting up that detailed plan, and ensuring that your goals are grounded in reality.

As the New Moon graces the celestial stage, it brings a potent opportunity for fresh beginnings. This lunar phase marks the perfect time to plant the seeds of your intentions. The universe hands you a blank canvas to paint your dreams. You have the cosmic green light to manifest your desires, especially in the areas of your life illuminated by the New Moon's energy.

Moon ingress Aquarius: Now, as the Moon strides into Aquarius, you're in for a cosmic shift. Aquarius is all about innovation, independence, and embracing your individuality. You'll feel the urge to break free from the ordinary, connect with your tribe, and explore new horizons.

JANUARY WEEK ONE

☀ Brace yourself for a cosmic tidal wave of romance and dreamy vibes as Venus elegantly waltzes into Pisces. It's like a serenade from the universe, urging you to paint your world with empathy and affection.

♦ Hold on to your cosmic gear because when Mars locks horns with Pluto, it's a clash of titans in the cosmic arena. This celestial duel invokes an electrifying fusion of power and transformation.

☽ As the Moon pirouettes gracefully into Pisces, your emotional landscape transforms into a dreamscape, where intuition and introspection hold sway. It's inviting you to journey and connect with mystical dimensions.

◯ When the Sun and Saturn engage in a harmonious sextile, it's as if the cosmic maestro directs a symphony of achievement and stability. The universe nods approvingly at your unwavering diligence and dedication.

✦ Prepare for a refreshing cosmic shift as the Moon charges headlong into Aries. This celestial spark lights a fire under your passions and fuels your drive.

JANUARY WEEK TWO

☿ Mercury's entrance into Capricorn marks a significant shift in how you approach communication and decision-making. It's as if your mental processes are now donning a practical and strategic suit. With thoughts grounded in the long-term, you'll find yourself carefully considering your goals and ambitions.

☽ The Moon's transition into Gemini ushers in an air of curiosity and sociability. Conversations become lively, and your thirst for knowledge is insatiable. Engaging in stimulating dialogues, learning new skills, and connecting are favored activities during this lunar phase.

☽ As the Moon moves into Cancer, emotions take center stage. You may seek to spend quality time with family and loved ones or create a cozy haven. This lunar position reminds you of the importance of self-care and close relationships, encouraging emotional well-being.

♂ The harmonious trine between Mars and Neptune introduces an intriguing blend of assertiveness and intuition. This alignment empowers your creative endeavors and spiritual pursuits.

JANUARY WEEK TWO

⚡ The Sun's trine with Uranus electrifies your existence with a thirst for change and innovation. It's as though the universe is sending a surge of revolutionary energy your way. You're open to embracing new experiences, unconventional ideas, and exciting opportunities.

🌕 The Full Moon, a celestial spectacle, shines its radiant light upon your accomplishments and aspirations. It's a moment of culmination and reflection, where you can bask in the glow of your achievements while reassessing your path. This lunar phase invites you to celebrate your successes and adjust your course if necessary.

🌙 As the Moon gracefully enters Leo, your inner performer takes center stage. Whether through artistic endeavors, public speaking, or simply sharing your unique talents, this lunar position encourages you to let your light shine brightly.

✨ Venus squares Jupiter, creating a celestial tug-of-war between indulgence and moderation. This aspect serves as a reminder to savor the richness of life while keeping a watchful eye on excesses.

JANUARY WEEK THREE

When the Sun opposes Mars, it's as if the cosmic stage is set for a showdown between ego and action. Tensions run high as you grapple with assertiveness and desires. Finding a harmonious balance between your drive and the need for compromise becomes the cosmic challenge.

The Moon's ingress into meticulous Virgo ushers in a time of increased attention to detail and a desire for order. You'll find satisfaction in caring for practical matters and improving efficiency in your daily routines.

The Sun's sextile with Neptune brings a gentle magic touch to your life. Your intuition and creativity flow harmoniously, making it a favorable moment for artistic pursuits and connecting with your inner muse.

Venus joins hands with Saturn in conjunction, creating a cosmic alliance that emphasizes commitment and responsibility in your relationships. This aspect encourages you to take your bonds seriously and work on building lasting foundations.

JANUARY WEEK THREE

🌙 As the Moon moves into gracious Libra, balance, and harmony, permeate your emotions. You'll have a heightened appreciation for beauty and diplomacy, seeking peace and fairness in your interactions.

📖 Mercury forms harmonious sextiles with Saturn and Venus, fostering transparent and thoughtful communication in your relationships. This alignment supports productive discussions and decision-making.

☀️ The Sun's ingress into Aquarius marks a shift towards innovative thinking and a desire for intellectual exploration. Your focus turns to community and humanitarian endeavors as you seek to make a meaningful impact.

☀️ The Sun's conjunction with Pluto intensifies your personal power and transformational potential. During this cosmic event, you're encouraged to dive deep into self-discovery and embrace your inner strength.

🌙 The Moon's transition into Scorpio adds a touch of intensity to your emotions. You'll find yourself drawn to deeper, more profound experiences and may uncover hidden truths as you navigate the emotional depths.

JANUARY WEEK FOUR

Mars forms a harmonious sextile with Uranus, sparking a surge of dynamic and innovative energy. It's a cosmic jolt that motivates you to break free from routines and enthusiastically explore new approaches.

Mercury's trine with Uranus brings a touch of genius to your thinking. It is a fantastic time for brainstorming and embracing your inner maverick.

The Moon's ingress into adventurous Sagittarius fuels your desire for exploration and knowledge. You'll crave new experiences and may find yourself planning exciting journeys, whether physical or intellectual.

Venus trines Mars, igniting passion and harmony in your relationships. It's like a cosmic dance of attraction and desire, encouraging you to express your affections.

Mercury's sextile with Neptune enhances intuition and creativity. Your imagination flows effortlessly, allowing you to express thoughts with poetic grace.

Venus sextiles Uranus, bringing excitement and novelty to your social life and relationships. You may feel drawn to spontaneous and thrilling activities.

JANUARY WEEK FOUR

☾ Mercury's ingress into Aquarius inspires progressive and forward-thinking ideas. Your communication style becomes more unconventional, and you'll enjoy exploring cutting-edge concepts.

☽ The Moon's ingress into Aquarius further emphasizes your desire for freedom and individuality. You'll be drawn to like-minded individuals who share your visionary outlook.

✷ Mercury's conjunction with Pluto delves into the depths of your thoughts and conversations. It's a time of profound insights and transformative communication.

● The New Moon marks a fresh beginning, offering an opportunity to set new intentions and plant seeds.

☾ The Moon's ingress into Pisces enhances your emotional sensitivity and intuition. You may experience vivid dreams and heightened empathy.

☀ The Sun's trine with Jupiter radiates positivity and abundance in a celestial blessing that amplifies your optimism and enthusiasm.

FEBRUARY WEEK ONE

♥ When Venus forms a conjunction with Neptune, the celestial stage is set for a romantic masterpiece. Love and affection take on an enchanting and otherworldly quality, akin to a celestial ballet where hearts entwine under a starry sky. This cosmic alignment inspires you to embrace your inner poet, allowing your affections to flow with artistic grace. It's a time when dreams and reality blur, inviting you to explore the depths of your emotions and express your love in ethereal ways.

☽ As the Moon gracefully ushers in the spirited Aries, your emotions catch fire with passionate and assertive energy. This lunar shift ignites your inner warrior, fueling desires with courage and vigor.

💬 Mercury's harmonious trine with expansive Jupiter opens the doors to intellectual horizons that stretch as far as the eye can see. Your mind is a tapestry of wisdom and optimism, making conversations flow with infectious enthusiasm.

☽ As the Moon finds solace in grounded Taurus, your emotions seek comfort in life's pleasures. This lunar placement encourages a tranquil haven of contentment.

FEBRUARY WEEK ONE

🍃 With Venus gracefully waltzing into Aries, your love life and personal style take on a bold and independent flair. This cosmic shift encourages you to express your desires with fearless determination.

⏩ Jupiter's direct motion acts as a cosmic green light, signaling a period of forward momentum and expansion. Projects and plans that may have felt momentarily stalled are now free to progress with renewed vigor.

🌙 As the Moon glides into versatile Gemini, your social interactions and intellectual curiosity emerge. Your communication skills shine, and you'll find joy in connecting with a diverse range of people, exploring new ideas, and engaging in lively conversations.

💜 Venus's sextile with transformative Pluto adds depth and intensity to your relationships and desires. It's as if your emotional connections enter a realm of profound transformation, encouraging you to explore the intricate layers of your links and dive fearlessly into the depths of passion. This cosmic embrace invites you to surrender to the mysteries of love with unwavering intensity.

FEBRUARY WEEK TWO

☽ As the Moon gracefully enters the nurturing waters of Cancer, your emotions take on a compassionate and intuitive quality. It's as if you're wrapped in a cosmic, comforting embrace, encouraging you to prioritize self-care and connect with your innermost feelings. Home and family become central themes during this lunar phase, making it an ideal time to create a warm and harmonious atmosphere.

○ When the Sun aligns with Mercury, your mind is illuminated with clarity and insight. This cosmic conjunction enhances communication, allowing your thoughts to flow seamlessly. It's a perfect time for expressing ideas, making important decisions, or engaging in intellectual pursuits.

● Mars forms a harmonious trine with Saturn, infusing your actions with a powerful sense of discipline and determination. This cosmic alliance gives you the endurance and focus to tackle even the most challenging tasks. It's like having a heavenly green light to pursue your goals with unwavering commitment.

FEBRUARY WEEK TWO

⚡ When the Sun squares Uranus, you may encounter unexpected disruptions and a longing for change. This cosmic clash challenges you to break free from routine and embrace innovation. While it can be a bit chaotic, it also offers the potential for exciting breakthroughs.

● The Full Moon casts a brilliant light on your accomplishments and illuminates your path. It's a time of culmination and reflection, where you can celebrate your achievements and release what no longer serves you.

☽ The Moon's transition into meticulous Virgo enhances your attention to detail and organizational skills. You'll find satisfaction in fine-tuning your daily routines and focusing on practical matters.

💬 On Valentine's Day, Mercury gracefully enters Pisces, infusing your thoughts and conversations with empathy and compassion. It's like a cosmic love note, encouraging heartfelt and soulful connections. During this romantic period, you'll naturally be able to convey your emotions and connect with others on a deeply spiritual level.

FEBRUARY WEEK THREE

☽ When the Moon gracefully enters charming Libra, it's as if the cosmic scales tip towards harmony and balance in your emotional world. Your feelings become attuned to fairness and aesthetics, and you're likely to appreciate the beauty in your surroundings. During this lunar phase, cultivating peace and equilibrium in your relationships takes center stage as you seek to create an atmosphere of serenity and cooperation.

☽ As the Moon delves deeper into the enigmatic waters of Scorpio, your emotional landscape takes on a profound and reflective quality. It's as though a cosmic spotlight shines on the hidden realms of life and your innermost desires. This phase encourages you to embrace emotional authenticity and explore the depths of your psyche, potentially leading to transformative insights. This lunar shift invites exploration of the hidden realms of your inner world and the mysteries of life itself. You'll likely experience heightened intuition and a desire to delve beneath the surface, seeking emotional authenticity and transformative experiences. It's a phase when you're unafraid to confront deeper truths and embrace the profound aspects of existence.

FEBRUARY WEEK THREE

◯ With the Sun's transition into compassionate Pisces, you embark on a journey of heightened sensitivity and artistic inspiration. Pisces, ruled by dreamy Neptune, invites you to immerse yourself in imagination and intuition. You'll feel a stronger connection to the collective consciousness, and activities such as creative expression, meditation, or spiritual pursuits are particularly favored during this time.

☽ As the Moon ventures into adventurous Sagittarius, optimism and a thirst for exploration fill the emotional landscape. You're drawn to new experiences, philosophical insights, and the quest for higher knowledge. This lunar phase encourages you to expand your mental and physical horizons as you embrace a spirit of freedom and intellectual growth.

◌ Mercury's square with expansive Jupiter brings enthusiasm and big thinking to your communication. It's as if your ideas are bursting with potential, and you're eager to share them with the world. However, this cosmic alignment also carries a cautionary note, reminding you to balance your visionary thinking with a healthy dose of practicality.

FEBRUARY WEEK FOUR

🌙 As the Moon gracefully moves into steadfast Capricorn, you'll find your emotions taking on a more disciplined and pragmatic tone. This lunar phase encourages you to set your sights on your goals and embrace a sense of responsibility. You'll have a heightened appreciation for structure and organization, making it an excellent time to tackle tasks that require diligence and focus. The Moon in Capricorn inspires you to pursue your ambitions with determination and to build a solid foundation for future success.

● Mars, the planet of action and energy, finally turns direct, ending a period of introspection and delayed progress. With Mars now in forward motion, you'll feel a renewed sense of vitality and motivation. It's as if a cosmic green light has been lit, allowing you to pursue your desires and projects with increased vigor. Your determination and drive will serve you well as you channel this direct Mars energy to accomplishing goals.

🌙 As the Moon enters the intellectually charged sign of Aquarius, your emotions may crave innovation. During this lunar phase, you feel a sense of community and a willingness to contribute to group efforts.

FEBRUARY WEEK FOUR

◌ Mercury's conjunction with Saturn adds a touch of seriousness and deliberation to your thoughts and communication. Your mental faculties are highly focused and disciplined, allowing you to tackle complex tasks and engage in meaningful discussions. It's an ideal time for structured thinking and long-term planning.

🌙 The Moon's transition into dreamy Pisces invites you to dive into the depths of your emotions and embrace your intuitive side. Your intuition is heightened, and you may find solace in artistic or spiritual pursuits.

◌ Mercury's sextile with Uranus adds an element of excitement and innovation to your mental processes. You'll be open to unconventional ideas and may have sudden flashes of insight. This cosmic combination encourages you to think outside the box and explore new intellectual horizons. It's a favorable time for creative problem-solving and exploring innovative solutions.

🌑 The New Moon marks a fresh start and a powerful opportunity for setting new intentions. As you embrace this lunar energy, consider what you wish to manifest and bring into your world.

MARCH WEEK ONE

Venus, the planet of love and relationships, embarks on its retrograde journey, signaling a period of reflection and reevaluation in matters of the heart. This cosmic twist encourages you to revisit past relationships, review your values, and reconsider your approach to love and partnerships. It's a time to focus on self-love and inner harmony, allowing you to emerge from this retrograde with a deeper understanding of your heart's desires.

Mercury's conjunction with Neptune creates a dreamy and imaginative atmosphere in your communication and thoughts. Your mind is attuned to the subtle realms of intuition and creativity. It's a moment when words can take on a poetic and artistic quality, making it an ideal time for creative expression, spiritual insights, and heartfelt conversations.

The Sun's square with Jupiter amplifies your optimism and enthusiasm but may also lead to a touch of overconfidence. While it's a moment for dreaming big and setting high goals, balancing your grand visions with practical considerations is essential. This cosmic aspect encourages you to aim high while staying grounded in your approach.

MARCH WEEK ONE

☽ As the Moon moves into sensual Taurus, your emotional landscape becomes rooted in comfort and practicality. You'll find solace in simple pleasures, from savoring delicious meals to indulging in sensory experiences. It's a time when emotional stability and security take precedence, and you may seek to create a harmonious and cozy environment.

☾ The Moon's transition into communicative Gemini amplifies your curiosity and desire for intellectual exploration. Conversations flow effortlessly, and you'll relish connecting with various people who stimulate your mind and expand your horizons.

☾ Mercury's sextile with transformative Pluto adds depth and intensity to your thoughts and conversations. This cosmic connection encourages you to delve fearlessly into the profound realms of understanding and connection. Your words carry a transformative power, and you're drawn to explore the mysteries of life and human nature with enthusiasm and authenticity.

☽ As the Moon finds its way into nurturing Cancer, emotions have a compassionate and protective quality.

MARCH WEEK TWO

☉ When the Sun forms a harmonious trine with Mars, you'll experience a boost of energy and enthusiasm. This cosmic alignment infuses your actions with confidence and vitality, making it an excellent time for assertive and dynamic endeavors. A strong sense of self-assuredness supports your ambitions, and you're ready to take on challenges with determination.

☾ As the Moon gracefully enters Leo, your emotions take on a regal and expressive quality. You'll feel a strong desire for attention and the spotlight. This lunar phase encourages you to embrace your inner performer and showcase your unique talents and creativity.

☿ Mercury's conjunction with Venus marks a period of harmonious and delightful communication. Your words and expressions are charming and diplomatic, making it a perfect time for romantic conversations and social interactions. Your prudent approach and pleasant demeanor can help you navigate relationships with ease.

☾ The Moon's transition into practical Virgo encourages attention to detail and a focus on organization. It's an ideal time for improving efficiency.

MARCH WEEK TWO

☼ When the Sun conjoins with Saturn, it's a time for increased discipline and focus. This aspect invites you to take responsibility for your actions and long-term goals. You'll feel a strong sense of duty and may be drawn to structured pursuits.

◐ The Full Moon shines a light on your achievements and long-term goals, allowing you to celebrate your successes and reevaluate your ambitions. It's a time to ensure that your aspirations align with your true desires and make any necessary adjustments.

◯ The Sun's sextile with Uranus brings an element of surprise and innovation to your life. While it can lead to unexpected changes or opportunities, it's also a chance to embrace individuality and break free from limitations. This aspect encourages you to welcome positive change and explore new horizons.

☾ As the Moon continues its journey into harmonious Libra, your emotional landscape takes on a diplomatic and relational tone. You'll naturally seek balance and harmony in your interactions and surroundings. It's ideal for promoting cooperation in your relationships.

MARCH WEEK THREE

🔄 Mercury's retrograde journey invites you to step back and reflect on your thoughts and communication. It's a time when misunderstandings and miscommunications may arise, so double-check your messages and be patient with delays. Use this cosmic pause to revisit old ideas and reevaluate your plans before moving forward.

☾ As the Moon moves into Scorpio, your emotions take on a more intense and mysterious quality. You'll find yourself delving into the depths of your feelings, seeking to uncover hidden truths within yourself and your relationships. This lunar phase encourages transformation and regeneration on an emotional level. This lunar phase enables you to embrace a spirit of exploration and seek knowledge that broadens your perspective.

♐ When the Moon enters adventurous Sagittarius, your emotions take flight, and you'll be drawn to explore new horizons. It's when you seek freedom and purpose in your experiences. The call for adventure is strong, and you'll find joy in embracing a more spontaneous and open-minded approach to life.

MARCH WEEK THREE

☀ The Sun's conjunction with Neptune marks a heightened sensitivity and spiritual connection phase. Your intuition is strong, and you'll find solace in creative and artistic pursuits. This cosmic alignment encourages compassion and a deep connection to the mystical and dreamy realms.

☺ The Sun's ingress into Aries heralds the Vernal Equinox, a time of renewal and fresh beginnings. Aries season brings a burst of energy and a sense of initiative. It's a time to embrace your individuality and take the lead in pursuing your goals and desires. As the days grow longer, you'll feel a growing sense of vitality and enthusiasm for what lies ahead.

💕 Venus's sextile with Pluto deepens your relationships and intensifies your passions. This cosmic connection encourages you to explore the depths of your desires and foster profound bonds with others. It's a magnetic influence that invites you to embrace the transformative power of love and intimacy. Your passions and attractions take on a profound quality, increasing the growth and transformation of your connections. 🌙 🔮

MARCH WEEK FOUR

☾ When the Moon gracefully enters the earthy realm of Capricorn, you'll notice a significant shift in your emotional landscape. Your feelings become grounded and focused, leading you to prioritize your responsibilities and long-term goals. During this lunar phase, there's a distinct satisfaction in taking care of your commitments to achieve your aims.

♣ The conjunction of the Sun and Venus infuses your life with an aura of romance and harmony. It's as if the cosmic spotlight shines on your relationships and the things that warm your heart. During this period, your interactions are characterized by affection and an appreciation for beauty in all its forms. This alignment creates the perfect atmosphere to express feelings and cherish life's finer moments.

✦ The Sun's sextile with Pluto deepens your experiences, adding a layer of intensity and transformation to your path. This cosmic connection prompts you to embrace change and take charge of your life. You're granted an opportunity to delve into the core of your desires, making meaningful changes and finding empowerment along the way.

MARCH WEEK FOUR

🌙 As the Moon journeys through Pisces, your emotional sensitivity and intuition take center stage. This cosmic transition invites you to immerse yourself in the world of dreams, creativity, and spiritual connection. You might discover solace in artistic or meditative pursuits, and your compassion for others reaches new heights.

● The Black Moon's ingress into Scorpio triggers a period of introspection and self-discovery. It encourages you to delve into the depths of your psyche, confronting any unresolved issues or hidden aspects of your personality.

✺ Venus's arrival in Pisces adds a touch of romantic idealism to your relationships. Your capacity for compassion and understanding deepens, creating a favorable environment for emotional connection and spiritual bonding. Kindness and selflessness take on a new level of beauty and significance.

💝 The conjunction of Venus and Neptune intensifies the dreamy and romantic ambiance. Your imagination soars, and you will likely be drawn to artistic and spiritual pursuits.

APRIL WEEK ONE

With the Moon's gentle shift into Cancer, your emotions take on a nurturing and empathetic quality. During this lunar phase, you're inclined to focus on home and family matters. The desire for emotional security and a strong connection with loved ones becomes prominent.

Saturn's sextile with Uranus introduces a harmonious cosmic dance between tradition and innovation. This alignment encourages you to embrace innovation within the framework of established structures.

Mars, in a harmonious sextile with Uranus, fuels your ambitions and stirs the desire for action and excitement. This cosmic alliance imbues you with the courage to pursue your goals with a bold and unconventional approach. It's a time for groundbreaking endeavors and taking risks with confidence.

Mars' trine with Saturn adds an element of discipline and focus to your actions. This cosmic combination brings a strong work ethic and the perseverance to overcome obstacles. You'll find energy is channeled efficiently, allowing you to progress objectives.

APRIL WEEK ONE

☽ The Moon's transition into Leo ignites a sense of self-expression and creativity. You're drawn to the spotlight during this lunar phase and may seek recognition.

☉ When the Sun forms a harmonious sextile with Jupiter, the cosmic energies smile upon your endeavors. This alignment brings optimism, enhancing confidence and expanding growth opportunities.

💖 Venus' trine with Mars adds a touch of romance and passion to your relationships and personal life. This harmonious connection fosters an atmosphere of harmony and affection, making it an ideal time to connect with loved ones and pursue desires with charm.

♣ The conjunction of Venus and Saturn introduces a period of relationship stability and commitment. It's as if the universe emphasizes enduring connections and the responsibilities that come with them. Your relationships may take on a more serious tone, and you're willing to invest time and effort in them.

🔄 With Mercury's direct motion, the cosmic fog of miscommunication and delays begins to clear. This period marks a return to straightforward conversations.

APRIL WEEK TWO

✦ When Venus forms a sextile with Uranus, it's like a cosmic invitation to infuse your relationships and appreciation of beauty with excitement and unpredictability. This harmonious alignment encourages you to embrace unique and unconventional forms of love and artistry. You may be drawn to individuals who exude an air of individuality and independence in your relationships. Creatively, you'll be inspired to experiment with fresh and avant-garde expressions of your artistic talents. This aspect can usher in pleasant surprises and new experiences in heart matters.

☽ As the Moon gracefully transitions into Virgo, you'll notice a shift towards a more analytical and detail-oriented emotional state. During this lunar phase, you may feel compelled to bring order to your surroundings and daily routines. Practical concerns and a desire for efficiency become paramount, leading you to tackle tasks with a sense of precision. You'll find emotional fulfillment in taking care of life's little details.

♥ Moving into Libra, the Moon encourages you to embrace harmony, balance, and diplomacy in your emotional landscape and relationships.

APRIL WEEK TWO

◗ The Full Moon, with its radiant glow, illuminates your path and highlights the achievements and culminations in your life. This celestial event marks a decisive moment of clarity and culmination. It's a time to acknowledge and celebrate the results of your hard work and intentions. Whether a personal goal or a relationship milestone, this is a time of reflection and acknowledgment.

※ As Venus turns direct, a fresh breeze of romantic and aesthetic renewal sweeps through your life. After introspection and revisiting matters of the heart, Venus embarks on a forward journey. Relationships regain their sense of momentum and clarity. You'll feel renewed passion and appreciation for beauty in all its forms. If there were any romantic or creative endeavors on hold, they are now infused with a sense of progress and positive momentum.

◗ With the Moon's ingress into Scorpio, this cosmic shift invites you to confront profound truths. This lunar phase encourages inner exploration and a willingness to dive beneath the surface. It's a time of emotional regeneration and transformation.

APRIL WEEK THREE

As the Moon enters adventurous and optimistic Sagittarius, your emotions take on a free-spirited and open-minded quality. It's like a cosmic invitation to explore, learn, and expand your horizons. You may find yourself craving adventure, whether that means embarking on a physical journey or diving into new intellectual pursuits. Embrace the sense of wanderlust and seek out experiences that broaden your perspective.

With Mercury's entrance into bold and fiery Aries, your communication style becomes assertive and direct. It's as if your words carry a spark of enthusiasm and courage. This placement fosters a pioneering spirit in your thoughts and ideas, making it an excellent time to start new projects or share your innovative concepts.

When Mercury aligns with dreamy Neptune, your mental landscape takes on a surreal and imaginative quality. It's like a cosmic poet's pen, allowing you to weave words and ideas into beautiful, ethereal tapestries. This aspect encourages creativity, intuition, and empathy in your communication. You may find yourself drawn to artistic or spiritual pursuits.

APRIL WEEK THREE

When Mercury forms a sextile with transformative Pluto, your communication becomes profound and insightful. It's as if you have a heightened ability to penetrate beneath the surface and uncover hidden truths. This aspect encourages deep and meaningful conversations that can lead to personal growth and transformation. Your words carry a weight of influence, making it a favorable time for research, psychological insights, or strategic planning.

As the Moon moves into independent and forward-thinking Aquarius, you may feel drawn to social causes, group activities, or unconventional approaches to problem-solving. This lunar phase fosters a sense of camaraderie and a desire to make a positive impact on the world.

When the Sun forms a square with Mars, there's a surge of dynamic energy that can lead to assertiveness and even conflict. This aspect encourages you to channel your energy constructively rather than impulsively. While challenges may arise, they also offer opportunities for growth and self-awareness. Be mindful of handling conflicts with diplomacy and patience.

APRIL WEEK FOUR

☾ As the Moon gently glides into Pisces, your emotions take on a dreamy and empathetic quality. It's a time when you may feel more attuned to the feelings of others and the subtle nuances of life. You'll find solace in introspective pursuits during this lunar phase.

☾ When the Sun squares Pluto, it's like a cosmic call for transformation and empowerment. This aspect stirs deep forces within you, encouraging you to confront power dynamics and embrace change. While it may bring challenges, it also offers the potential for rebirth.

💕 Venus's conjunction with Saturn adds a touch of seriousness to your relationships and creative endeavors. This aspect encourages commitment and the building of long-lasting connections. While it may bring some responsibilities, it also offers the stability and structure needed for lasting love and artistry.

◌ As the Moon enters Aries, your emotions take on a fiery and assertive quality. It's like a cosmic call to action, inspiring you to pursue your desires with enthusiasm and courage. Your competitive spirit is ignited, and you're ready to take on challenges.

APRIL WEEK FOUR

🔺 Mars opposing Pluto is a powerhouse of intensity and transformation. This aspect ignites a cosmic showdown between the warrior and the underworld. While challenging, it also offers the potential for profound change and healing.

🌑 The New Moon marks a fresh start and a blank canvas for your intentions. It's a time to set new goals and plant the seeds of your desires. This lunar phase is like a cosmic reset button, inviting you to manifest your dreams and embark on a growth journey.

🌗 As the Moon enters Gemini, your emotions take on a communicative and curious quality. It's a time when you crave mental stimulation and social interaction. You'll enjoy conversations and intellectual pursuits, as your mind is agile and versatile.

❁ Venus's ingress into Aries adds a burst of passion and independence to your relationships and creative expression. This celestial shift encourages you to embrace your desires and pursue what makes your heart sing. You're unapologetically yourself in matters of love and artistry, valuing spontaneity and individuality.

MAY WEEK ONE

🌙 As the Moon moves into nurturing Cancer, your emotions become deeply attuned to the needs of home and family. You may find solace in spending quality time with loved ones.

🌙 When Venus and Neptune come together in a dreamy conjunction, it's as if the realms of love and beauty merge with the mystical and ethereal. This celestial connection inspires profound romantic ideals and a heightened appreciation for art and aesthetics. You might lose yourself in a world of creative inspiration and boundless compassion.

☀ As the Moon transitions into radiant Leo, your emotions take on a more expressive and dramatic quality. It's a time when you seek recognition and the opportunity to shine. You may be drawn to creative and artistic pursuits that allow you to showcase your unique talents and personality.

🔄 When Pluto turns retrograde, it initiates a transformative journey within. This period encourages you to explore the depths of your psyche and address power dynamics in your life.

MAY WEEK ONE

📖 Mercury's harmonious sextile with Jupiter expands your mental horizons and encourages open-mindedness. It's a time when your thoughts are infused with optimism and a thirst for knowledge. This aspect supports learning, communication, and the sharing of big ideas.

🌙 With the Moon's transition into Virgo, your emotions take on a practical and analytical tone. You're inclined to pay attention to details, organize your environment, and focus on tasks that require precision. This lunar phase promotes efficiency and a desire for self-improvement.

💜 Venus's harmonious sextile with Pluto adds depth and intensity to your relationships and creative expressions. This celestial connection fosters emotional and transformative experiences in matters of the heart and artistic pursuits. You may be drawn to passionate connections and creative endeavors that touch the soul. It's like a cosmic invitation to explore the hidden facets of love and art. You're drawn to experiences that are transformative and emotionally profound. This aspect encourages passionate and meaningful connections.

MAY WEEK TWO

❁ When the Moon gracefully enters Libra, your emotions become attuned to the harmony, beauty, and balance in your surroundings. It's a cosmic invitation to seek equilibrium and peace in your relationships and daily life. This lunar phase encourages you to embrace diplomacy, express your appreciation for aesthetics, and work towards greater cooperation.

🌱 Mercury's transition into Taurus brings a grounded and practical approach to your thoughts and communication. Your mind becomes more focused on tangible matters, such as finances. This period supports transparent, deliberate, and systematic thinking, making it an excellent time for making solid plans and decisions. You're drawn to explore the mysteries of life, and you may find yourself more perceptive and emotionally resilient during this lunar phase.

🦂 As the Moon moves into Scorpio, your emotions take on a profound and transformative quality. You're drawn to explore the mysteries of life and delve into your inner psyche. This lunar phase encourages you to embrace your passions, confront your fears, and seek profound emotional connections.

MAY WEEK TWO

🌕 The Full Moon is a culmination of energy and a time to reap the rewards of your efforts. It's like a cosmic spotlight illuminating the results of your intentions and actions from the previous New Moon. This phase encourages you to release what no longer serves you and celebrate your achievements.

🔍 Mercury's square with Pluto intensifies your thoughts and communication. It's when your mind delves into deep, often hidden, matters. While this can bring insights and powerful transformations, it can also lead to intense debates and power struggles. Use this energy to uncover truths and promote healing communication. It's essential to choose your words wisely and use this energy for positive change.

♐ As the Moon transitions into Sagittarius, your emotions become adventurous and freedom-seeking. You're eager to expand your horizons, both physically and mentally. This lunar phase encourages you to embrace optimism, engage in philosophical exploration, and explore new horizons through travel or learning.

MAY WEEK THREE

🔺 When the Moon gracefully transitions into Capricorn, your emotions adopt a practical and responsible demeanor. You're inclined to focus on your goals, career, and long-term ambitions. This lunar phase encourages discipline, hard work, and a desire for tangible results.

⚡ The conjunction of the Sun and Uranus brings a surge of innovation and unexpected changes. It's like a cosmic lightning bolt, shaking your life and inspiring you to break free from routines. It encourages you to embrace uniqueness, take risks, and explore new possibilities.

🔔 Mercury's square with Mars creates a dynamic and assertive atmosphere in your communication. You're ready to express your thoughts and ideas, but there's a potential for arguments and impulsive speech. Choosing your words carefully and channeling your mental energy is essential.

🏺 As the Moon moves into Aquarius, your emotions become more progressive and open-minded. You're inclined to seek intellectual stimulation and connect with like-minded individuals. This lunar phase encourages a sense of community.

MAY WEEK THREE

The Sun's sextile with Saturn is a harmonious alignment that brings stability and a sense of accomplishment. It's like a cosmic pat on the back for your hard work and dedication. This aspect encourages you to set realistic goals, make steady progress, and confidently take on leadership roles.

As the Moon enters Pisces, your emotions take on a dreamy and intuitive quality. It's like a cosmic lullaby, encouraging introspection and a connection to the mystical realms. This lunar shift opens the door to profound sensitivity, artistic inspiration, and a deeper understanding of your inner world.

The Sun's ingress into Gemini marks a shift towards curiosity, communication, and versatility. You become more mentally agile and eager to explore various interests. This solar phase encourages you to engage in conversations, expand your knowledge, and approach life with a playful and adaptable mindset. You become more flexible, curious, and eager to learn as it's a time of mental stimulation and versatility.

MAY WEEK FOUR

 The Sun sextile with Neptune bathes your life in a dreamy and intuitive glow. It's as if the boundaries between reality and imagination blur, allowing for heightened creativity and a deeper connection to your spiritual side. This aspect encourages empathy, artistic inspiration, and a sense of enchantment.

 When the Sun forms a trine with Pluto, it's like a cosmic invitation to embrace transformation and empowerment. You have the strength to make profound changes in your life and radiate a sense of authority and self-confidence. Align your desires with your power and create lasting transformations.

 Mercury's conjunction with Uranus ignites your mind with innovative and unconventional ideas. You're open to new perspectives and may have sudden insights that lead to groundbreaking discoveries. This aspect encourages intellectual excitement and a desire to break from conventional thinking.

 Saturn's ingress into Aries marks a significant shift. Aries' influence encourages you to take initiative and assert yourself in pursuing your goals.

MAY WEEK FOUR

Mercury's sextile with Saturn brings a practical and disciplined approach to your thinking and communication. You can express your ideas with clarity and structure, making it an excellent time for planning and serious discussions.

The New Moon marks a fresh beginning and a time to set new intentions. It's like a cosmic reset button, encouraging you to plant the seeds of your desires and embark on new journeys. This lunar phase fosters introspection and the formulation of goals.

Mercury's trine with Pluto intensifies your mental processes and communication. You can delve deep into complex subjects and uncover hidden information. This aspect promotes transformative conversations and a desire to get to the heart of matters.

The Sun's conjunction with Mercury illuminates your thinking and self-expression. You spotlight your ideas and communication style, making it an excellent time to share your thoughts as you can express yourself with confidence and precision.

JUNE WEEK ONE

❈ When the Moon gracefully enters Virgo, your emotions take on a practical and analytical tone. It's a time when you seek order, organization, and attention to detail. Your nurturing instincts may lead you to focus on acts of service and improving your immediate environment. This lunar phase encourages you to refine your daily routines and embrace a sense of efficiency and health.

🌄 As the Moon transitions into Libra, your emotions seek balance, harmony, and a sense of fairness. You're more inclined to prioritize cooperation and diplomacy in your relationships. This lunar phase encourages you to find common ground, connect with others, and appreciate the beauty in your surroundings.

💚 Venus sextile Jupiter creates a harmonious dance of love and abundance. Your relationships and financial matters receive a touch of luck and expansion. This aspect encourages feelings of joy, generosity, and an appreciation for the finer things in life. This aspect promotes optimism and generosity.

JUNE WEEK ONE

🚀 Mercury sextile Mars ignites your mental and communicative prowess. Your thinking is sharp, and you have the energy and assertiveness to express your ideas with confidence. This aspect encourages effective and dynamic communication, making it an excellent time for discussions and decision-making.

🌷 Venus's ingress into Taurus marks a sensual and stabilizing shift in your love life and personal style. You're drawn to life's pleasures, comfort, and the finer things. This transit encourages you to indulge in sensory experiences and appreciate the beauty that surrounds you.

🌲 When the Moon delves into Scorpio, your emotions take on an intense and passionate quality. You're inclined to explore deep-seated feelings and uncover hidden truths. This lunar phase encourages you to embrace transformation and delve into the mysteries of life, both within and around you. You're drawn to explore the mysteries of life, delve into psychological matters, and embrace transformation. This lunar phase encourages self-reflection and a willingness to go beneath the surface of your experiences.

JUNE WEEK TWO

Mercury's conjunction with Jupiter is like a mental burst of brilliance. Your mind is open, expansive, and eager to explore new horizons. This aspect fosters optimism, a love for learning, and the ability to grasp complex concepts with ease.

With Mercury's move into Cancer, your thoughts and communication take on a nurturing and emotionally sensitive tone. You're more attuned to the needs of those around you, and your words carry a comforting, empathetic quality. It's a time when your mind seeks emotional connections and a sense of security.

Mercury square Saturn challenges your mental agility and communication. You may encounter obstacles or delays in expressing your ideas, requiring patience and precision. This aspect encourages you to structure your thoughts and plans methodically.

Venus square Pluto brings intensity and transformation to your relationships and values. This aspect can stir up power struggles and intense emotions in your love life. It encourages you to address deeper issues and let go of what no longer serves your growth.

JUNE WEEK TWO

🏠 Jupiter's ingress into Cancer marks a shift in the cosmic landscape. It's a time when expansion and growth are linked to home, family, and emotional well-being. Jupiter in Cancer encourages you to find abundance and opportunity through nurturing and protective qualities.

🌕 The Full Moon is a culmination of energy and emotions. It's a time when your goals and intentions come to fruition or when you may need to let go of what no longer serves you. This lunar phase encourages you to reflect on your achievements and make adjustments.

💚 Mercury's sextile with Venus brings ease and charm to your communication and social interactions. You'll find it natural to express your affection and appreciation, making it an excellent time for heartfelt conversations and harmonious connections.

🏔️ As the Moon enters Capricorn, your emotions adopt a practical and responsible tone. This lunar phase encourages you to focus on your long-term goals, career, and matters of structure and discipline.

JUNE WEEK THREE

🍂 Mars square Uranus sets the stage for a high-energy and potentially volatile cosmic dance. It's like a clash of the titans as the impulsive and daring qualities of Mars challenge the unpredictable and rebellious nature of Uranus. This aspect can bring sudden disruptions and a strong urge for freedom and change. Caution and awareness are essential during this electrifying phase.

🌕 Jupiter square Saturn forms a dynamic alignment that combines expansion and restriction. It's as if the cosmic teacher (Saturn) and the cosmic optimist (Jupiter) engage in a tug-of-war. This aspect encourages you to find the balance between growth and discipline, allowing you to make sustainable progress toward your goals.

🌙 With the Moon's graceful ingress into Pisces, your emotions take on a dreamy and intuitive quality.

💧 As Mars moves into Virgo, your energy becomes more precise and detail-oriented. It's like a cosmic call to focus on the specifics of your goals and tasks. This transit encourages you to apply your energy diligently, pay attention to health and wellness, and take care of the finer points of your daily life.

JUNE WEEK THREE

🔺 When the Moon shifts into Aries, your emotions become fiery and action-oriented. You'll feel a surge of motivation and a desire to take the lead. This lunar phase encourages you to embrace new beginnings, be assertive in your pursuits, and pursue your goals with enthusiasm.

🌒 Jupiter square Neptune creates a hazy and somewhat confusing cosmic atmosphere. It's like a meeting between boundless optimism (Jupiter) and elusive dreams (Neptune). This aspect encourages you to be cautious in matters of faith and idealism, as it can lead to misplaced trust or illusions. Ground your dreams in practicality.

🌿 As the Moon moves into Taurus, your emotions adopt a stable and sensual quality.

☀️ As the Sun enters Cancer, you welcome the June Solstice. This event marks the official start of summer in the Northern Hemisphere and winter in the Southern Hemisphere. It's a time of illumination and heightened awareness. Cancer encourages you to focus on home and family and nurture your emotional bonds.

JUNE WEEK FOUR

🚀 Mars sextile Jupiter is a burst of energy and enthusiasm. It's like a cosmic rocket fueling your actions with confidence and optimism. This aspect encourages you to take bold steps toward your goals and embrace new opportunities with a sense of adventure.

⌛ When the Sun forms a square with Saturn, you may encounter obstacles and limitations that test your patience and perseverance. This aspect is like a cosmic reality check, urging you to approach your responsibilities and commitments with discipline.

☺ Sun conjunct Jupiter is a powerful aspect of expansion and growth. It's like a cosmic green light illuminating your path to success and abundance. This aspect encourages you to have confidence in your abilities and to dream big, as opportunities for advancement and good fortune abound.

🌑 The New Moon marks a fresh beginning and a time to set new intentions. It's like a cosmic blank canvas, inviting you to plant the seeds of your desires and aspirations. This lunar phase encourages you to visualize your goals and take steps toward realization.

JUNE WEEK FOUR

✒ Mercury sextile Uranus adds a touch of innovation to your communication style. It's like a cosmic lightning bolt, sparking inventive ideas and intellectual breakthroughs. This aspect encourages you to think outside the box and explore unconventional solutions.

💧 Sun sextile Mars infuses your actions with vitality and assertiveness. It's like a cosmic engine propelling you forward with determination and energy. This aspect encourages you to tackle challenges with courage and enthusiasm.

🦁 Mercury's move into Leo amplifies your communication with flair and creativity. You'll express yourself with confidence and a touch of drama, making your words and ideas stand out. This transit encourages you to share your unique perspective and shine in your verbal or written expressions.

⌛ Mercury trine Saturn is a harmonious aspect that bolsters your focus and discipline. It's like a cosmic blueprint for structured thinking and effective planning. This aspect encourages you to take a systematic approach to your tasks and responsibilities.

JULY WEEK ONE

🌙 As the Moon moves into Scorpio, your emotions take on an intense and probing quality. It's like a cosmic invitation to explore the depths of your feelings and uncover hidden truths. This lunar phase encourages you to embrace transformation and your inner power.

🌙 Venus's conjunction with Uranus brings unexpected and exciting developments in your relationships and values. It's like a cosmic spark that electrifies your love life and financial matters. This aspect encourages you to be open to unconventional connections.

❀ Venus's move into Gemini adds a light and social touch to your love and aesthetic preferences. It's like a cosmic breeze that encourages flirtation and a curious exploration of beauty. This transit brings a desire for variety and intellectual connections in your relationships and creative endeavors.

☾ Neptune's retrograde period begins, prompting a review of your dreams, intuition, and spiritual connection. It's inviting you to reflect on your ideals and illusions. This retrograde encourages you to discern between fantasy and reality.

JULY WEEK ONE

Venus's sextile with Neptune adds a touch of enchantment and romance to your relationships and artistic pursuits. It's like a cosmic watercolor painting, infusing your life with a dreamy and imaginative quality. This aspect encourages creative expression and a deep connection with your spiritual side.

The Moon's ingress into Sagittarius infuses your emotions with a sense of adventure and exploration. This lunar phase inspires a quest for knowledge and a thirst for freedom.

Uranus's ingress into Gemini marks a shift in innovative thinking and communication. It's like a cosmic upgrade to your mental processes, inspiring unique ideas and a desire for intellectual freedom. This transit encourages you to embrace change and stay open to exciting discoveries.

Venus's trine with Pluto brings transformative and passionate energy to your relationships and creative endeavors. It's like a cosmic cauldron of intensity and deep connection. This aspect encourages you to explore the depths of your emotions and strengthen bonds.

JULY WEEK TWO

🌙 When the Moon gracefully moves into Capricorn, you're prompted to embrace a more serious and responsible emotional demeanor. You'll find yourself inclined to focus on your long-term goals, ambitions, and obligations. This lunar placement encourages a sense of duty and a commitment to fulfilling your responsibilities, lending an air of determination to your emotional landscape.

🌕 The Full Moon, a celestial spectacle that occurs when the Moon opposes the Sun, marks a pivotal point in your emotional journey. It's a cosmic turning point, shining a radiant light on your achievements and emotions. During this phase, you'll feel the urge to assess what you've accomplished and celebrate your successes. It's a period of reflection and introspection, offering you the opportunity to let go of what no longer serves your highest good and to make space for new beginnings.

🌙 As the Moon transits into Aquarius, there's a refreshing breeze of independence and innovation that sweeps through your emotional landscape. This astrological shift is a cosmic catalyst, awakening your inner rebel and sparking a desire for unique experiences.

JULY WEEK TWO

⧗ Saturn turning retrograde is a significant cosmic event that initiates a period of introspection and review. This planet, often seen as the celestial taskmaster, invites you to revisit your responsibilities and long-term goals. During this retrograde, it's as if Saturn transforms into a cosmic teacher, encouraging you to scrutinize the structures of your life. This planetary shift is a time to ensure that your ambitions and aspirations align with your true desires and values. The retrograde period prompts you to evaluate your commitments and make any necessary adjustments.

☾ When the Moon wades into Pisces, the emotional landscape takes on a more sensitive quality. This astrological shift is akin to a cosmic artist applying vivid and dreamy hues to your feelings. During this phase, introspection becomes your companion, and you're encouraged to delve into the depths of your emotions. Compassion and a profound connection to your inner world become more pronounced. You may find solace in creative and artistic pursuits as the Piscean energy nurtures your imagination and intuition.

JULY WEEK THREE

☽ When the Moon transitions into Aries, there's an exhilarating cosmic energy that rushes in. It's as if a spark of inspiration ignites your emotional landscape, prompting you to embrace your adventurous side. During this lunar phase, your feelings are characterized by boldness, enthusiasm, and a strong urge to take the lead. It's the ideal time to initiate new projects or pursue your desires with fiery determination.

🔄 Mercury's retrograde motion invites you into a realm of introspection and revision. It's like a celestial storyteller pressing pause, encouraging you to reflect on your thoughts, ideas, and the way you connect with the world. This cosmic event prompts you to revisit past conversations, clarify misunderstandings, and fine-tune your thinking processes. It's an opportunity for self-discovery and improving your communication skills.

☽ As the Moon glides into Taurus, a profound sense of stability and grounding envelops your emotional world. During this lunar phase, your senses are heightened, and you may have an increased appreciation for life's simple pleasures.

JULY WEEK THREE

♥ The alignment between Mercury and Venus in a harmonious sextile creates a delightful cosmic harmony between your thoughts and emotions. It's as if your mind and heart engage in a beautifully synchronized dance. This aspect encourages warm, affectionate communication and fosters an ideal atmosphere for meaningful conversations and heartfelt expressions of love and appreciation.

☾ With the Moon's transition into Gemini, your emotional landscape takes on a curious and communicative tone. It's like a cosmic storyteller has awakened within you, urging you to share your feelings and ideas with the world. During this lunar phase, intellectual curiosity is at its peak, and you may find yourself craving engaging conversations and connections with others. Your mind is agile, and your heart is open to exploring the diversity of human interactions.

These celestial movements guide you through an array of emotional experiences; from the bold and adventurous spirit of Aries to the reflective pause of Mercury retrograde, you reveal opportunities for growth.

JULY WEEK FOUR

☼ The Sun's ingress into Leo marks a vibrant and dynamic cosmic shift. Leo, the sign of the lion, brings an air of regal confidence and self-expression to your life. As the Sun takes its throne in this fiery realm, you'll feel a surge of creativity, a desire to shine, and a playful spirit awakening within you.

When the Sun forms a harmonious sextile with Uranus, you're in for a dose of cosmic innovation and excitement. This aspect is like a jolt of electric energy, urging you to break free from the ordinary and embrace the extraordinary. You'll find it easier to express your individuality and infuse a touch of rebellion into your life. It's an ideal time for exploring new, unconventional ideas and pathways, sparking your curiosity and a desire to create positive change.

Venus square Mars stirs the cosmic pot of passion and desire. This celestial interaction can feel like a clash of the Titans as the planet of love, Venus, squares off with the planet of action, Mars. By understanding and managing this dynamic energy, you can harness it to fuel your passions and deepen your connections.

JULY WEEK FOUR

🌑 The arrival of the New Moon is like a blank canvas waiting to be painted with your desires and intentions. This lunar phase is the perfect time to set fresh goals and start new projects. The energy of the New Moon supports your visions for the future and invites you to plant the seeds of your aspirations. It's a time of renewal, and your intentions carry the promise of growth and transformation in the days and weeks to come.

🌑 When the Sun opposes Pluto, it's a celestial confrontation with the transformative forces of the universe. This aspect may stir deep-seated issues or power struggles. It's an opportunity to address any hidden aspects of your life and release what no longer serves you. While this aspect may feel intense, it also provides a chance for profound personal growth.

🌕 The Sun's conjunction with Mercury unites your conscious awareness with your thoughts and communication. You'll be more articulate and persuasive, allowing you to express your ideas with confidence and grace.

AUGUST WEEK ONE

💔 Venus square Saturn initiates a celestial challenge between love and responsibility that can feel like a tightrope walk in the realm of relationships. This aspect creates a cosmic tug-of-war between your desire for affection and the practical demands of life. It's as if you're balancing on a delicate scale, trying to find an equilibrium between your romantic longings and the need for structure. While it can bring about a sense of restriction and limitations, it's also an opportunity for you to define your boundaries and understand the importance of commitment in matters of the heart. Take this time to reflect on what you truly value in your connections and how to build lasting foundations.

🌙 Venus square Neptune adds an element of enchantment and confusion to the landscape of love. It's like dancing through a mystical fog, where the lines between reality and fantasy blur. This aspect can lead to idealization or misunderstandings in your relationships. Your heart might yearn for an idealized version of love, but it's crucial to maintain a level of clarity. Trust your intuition, but also ensure that your emotions are firmly anchored in reality.

AUGUST WEEK ONE

♐ With the Moon's ingress into Sagittarius, your emotions take flight on the wings of adventure. It's as if your heart is a free spirit craving new experiences and broader horizons. This lunar placement fuels your optimism and desire for personal growth. You're drawn to explore uncharted territory and expand your perspective on life. Seek opportunities for learning and embrace the thrill of discovery.

♑ As the Moon transitions into Capricorn, a more pragmatic and responsible emotional energy comes into play. During this phase, you're inclined to find satisfaction in accomplishing tasks, setting goals, and making strides in your professional life. The need for structure and organization becomes prominent, and you can channel your emotions into productive endeavors.

♎ Mars's ingress into Libra introduces a sense of equilibrium and diplomacy to your actions. This cosmic shift encourages you to approach conflicts with a graceful touch and a cooperative mindset. You recognize the value of harmony in your interactions and may find yourself mediating disputes or striving for peaceful resolutions.

AUGUST WEEK TWO

⚔ Mars's opposition to Saturn brings a clash between assertiveness and restraint. It's like a cosmic showdown between the warrior planet and the disciplinarian of the zodiac. You may feel as though your ambitions and desires are met with obstacles and delays, which can be frustrating. However, this aspect also provides an opportunity to fine-tune your goals and develop the patience and persistence needed to overcome challenges.

🌕 The Full Moon is a decisive moment of culmination and release. It's a time when the Sun in one sign opposes the Moon in the opposite sign, creating a sense of balance and tension. Emotions can run high during a Full Moon, and it often brings matters to a head. This lunar phase illuminates what was hidden and provides clarity on issues that have been brewing beneath the surface.

☾ Mars's opposition to Neptune adds a layer of mysticism and uncertainty to your actions and desires. You might feel a bit directionless or even experience disillusionment as your ambitions collide with illusions or confusing circumstances.

AUGUST WEEK TWO

◐ Mars's trine to Pluto is a powerhouse of transformative energy. It's as if you're given access to the depths of your inner power and determination. This aspect empowers you to tackle challenges and make lasting changes. A desire for profound transformation fuels your actions, and you're unafraid to confront issues that have been lurking in the shadows. This cosmic alignment supports your efforts to take control of your destiny.

🔄 Mercury turning direct signals a shift in communication and decision-making. After a period of introspection and review, you're now better equipped to move forward with your plans. It's a time for clearer thinking and more straightforward conversations. Be prepared for smoother negotiations and a sense of progress in your projects and endeavors.

♎ The sextile between Saturn and Uranus creates a harmonious blend of tradition and innovation. This aspect encourages you to find practical and realistic ways to implement changes in your life. You're able to balance your need for stability with a desire for progress, making it an ideal time for modernizing traditions.

AUGUST WEEK THREE

⚡ The harmonious sextile between Mercury and Mars is akin to having a pair of intellectual and communicative power tools at your disposal. During this celestial alignment, your thoughts and words are finely honed, as if the universe itself is sharpening your mental acuity and empowering your communication. It's an ideal time to tackle tasks that require both strategic thinking and proactive dialogue. Whether you're crafting plans, resolving problems, or engaging in conversations, you'll find your expressions infused with an extra dose of clarity and assertiveness.

☽ The Moon's journey through inquisitive Gemini brings an intellectual breeze into your life. It's as though your mind flings open the windows, eager to let in fresh ideas, information, and perspectives. This lunar influence nurtures your curiosity, making it the perfect time to engage in stimulating discussions, explore new subjects, and embrace the wealth of knowledge that surrounds you. Your mental faculties are agile, and you're keen to absorb all you can.

AUGUST WEEK THREE

✦ The reappearance of Mercury's sextile to Mars is akin to a cosmic encore performance. Your mental faculties continue to shine, bolstering your communicative prowess. With this aspect, you're not just expressing thoughts; you're wielding your words with conviction. It's a time for problem-solving with precision as mental clarity prevails.

☽ As the Moon enters nurturing Cancer, emotions move to center stage. It's as if the cosmic spotlight is now focused on matters of the heart and the hearth. This lunar placement ushers in an atmosphere of emotional connection, making it an excellent time for strengthening bonds with loved ones, tending to the home, and seeking comfort in the embrace of family.

✹ The Moon's passage through vibrant Leo introduces a touch of theatricality to your daily life. You'll find your inner performer awakened, drawing you towards self-expression, creative endeavors, and perhaps a bit of dramatic flair. This lunar influence encourages you to embrace your artistic side, share your unique talents, and revel in the spotlight. It's a time for infusing joy and letting your inner child revel in the joy of creativity.

AUGUST WEEK FOUR

☉ As the Sun gracefully enters Virgo, you'll find your focus shifting towards practical matters and the finer details of life. Your desire for order and precision is heightened, making it an ideal period to tackle tasks that require attention and dedication.

🌑 The arrival of the New Moon marks a fresh beginning in your life. It's like turning the page of a new chapter in your personal story. This lunar phase encourages you to set intentions, plant seeds for future growth, and embrace change. The energy of the New Moon is potent for starting projects or embarking on transformations.

⚡ When the Sun forms a square to Uranus, there's an electrifying charge in the air. You might feel an urge to break free from routines and explore new horizons. Unexpected events and opportunities can arise, challenging the status quo. While it may bring a degree of unpredictability, this aspect offers the chance for personal liberation and innovation.

✹ Venus' entrance into Leo ushers in a period of warmth, creativity, and self-expression in matters of the heart. You're inclined to seek fun and admiration.

AUGUST WEEK FOUR

💖 Venus forms a trine with Saturn, grounding your relationships with stability and commitment. It's a celestial reminder of the enduring connections in your life. You'll find joy in building lasting, meaningful partnerships, whether in love or business. This aspect brings responsibility and loyalty to your interactions.

✳ Venus' harmonious sextile to Uranus adds a touch of excitement and innovation to your relationships and creative pursuits. You're open to exploring new avenues for pleasure and connection. Unconventional or unique individuals may captivate your heart during this time.

💧 Venus' trine to Neptune deepens the romantic and dreamy vibes. Your relationships are infused with compassion, empathy, and a touch of magic. This aspect heightens your appreciation for beauty and encourages acts of kindness and generosity.

🌑 As Venus opposes Pluto, intense emotions may surface in your relationships. Power struggles and transformative experiences are possible. It's a time for deep self-reflection and understanding your desires on a profound level.

SEPTEMBER WEEK ONE

🪶 As Saturn makes its entrance into Pisces, you're embarking on a spiritual journey of profound introspection. Pisces is a sign that delves deep into emotions and intuition, and with Saturn's influence, you'll be compelled to explore your inner world. This period encourages you to develop greater empathy, understanding, and compassion, both for yourself and others. It's a time to reconsider your dreams, dive into creative and intuitive pursuits, and connect with your higher self.

📄 Mercury's transition into Virgo signifies a time of mental precision and analytical thinking. Virgo is known for its attention to detail, and this energy will enhance your problem-solving abilities and organizational skills. It's an excellent time for setting your life in order, focusing on health and wellness, and attending to the finer points of your daily routines.

⚡ When Mercury squares Uranus, you'll experience flashes of innovative thinking and potentially unexpected insights. This aspect can add a touch of restlessness to your mental state, encouraging you to break free from routine thought patterns.

SEPTEMBER WEEK ONE

☄ The Mars Jupiter square ignites a fire of enthusiasm and ambition. It's a phase where you'll feel the urge to expand your horizons and seek new adventures. While this energy can be incredibly motivating, be cautious not to overextend yourself. Balance is key. When managed wisely, this transition can lead to significant accomplishments and personal growth.

🔄 Uranus turning retrograde initiates a period of inner exploration. You'll review the changes and innovations you've encountered in recent months. This retrograde invites you to integrate newfound insights and extract deeper meaning from your experiences. It's a time to connect with your inner self and identify the unique path toward personal growth and liberation.

🌝 The Full Moon represents the climax of energy in the lunar cycle. It's the moment to harvest the results of your efforts and intentions set during the previous New Moon. Emotions can run high during this time, so use it as an opportunity for self-reflection, self-awareness, and personal growth. It's an excellent occasion to gain clarity and closure. Don't be afraid to delve deep into your psyche during this transformative period.

SEPTEMBER WEEK TWO

☽ As the Moon ushers in Aries, your emotions take on a vibrant, fiery quality. You'll find yourself brimming with enthusiasm and a strong desire to take the lead. This period is a perfect time to initiate new projects, assert your individuality, and boldly step into the forefront of your life's stage. It's an emotional spark that encourages you to embrace change and tackle challenges with a courageous spirit.

☽ Transitioning into Taurus, the Moon brings with it a sense of stability and practicality. During this time, your emotions lean towards seeking comfort, security, and the finer things in life. It's a phase that encourages you to indulge in life's sensual pleasures, nurture your relationships, and focus on financial matters. Your emotional landscape becomes anchored in the tangible and material world.

☉ The Sun's harmonious sextile with Jupiter illuminates your life with radiant optimism and a tapestry of opportunities. This celestial dance expands your horizons, both mentally and physically, making it a favorable time to set ambitious goals and pursue new adventures with unwavering confidence.

SEPTEMBER WEEK TWO

☽ When the Moon graces Gemini with its presence, your curiosity and sociability reach their peak. You'll find yourself drawn to a whirlwind of activities, conversations, and intellectual pursuits. It's a phase that encourages you to connect with others, learn new things, and engage in lively discussions. Your mind becomes a fertile ground for exploration and enlightenment.

✹ Mercury's harmonious sextile with Jupiter acts as a cosmic amplifier for your communication skills and intellectual abilities. Your words and thoughts flow with ease, and your ideas are met with enthusiasm. It's a splendid time for making plans, embarking on educational journeys, and sharing your insights with a broader audience. This celestial alliance inspires grand thinking and strategic vision.

☉ The Sun's conjunction with Mercury aligns your thoughts and self-expression in perfect harmony. Your intellect is sharp, and your ability to articulate your ideas is at its peak. This alignment bestows mental clarity and paves the way for meaningful conversations, profound revelations, and effective communication. It's as though the universe itself is guiding your words and thoughts.

SEPTEMBER WEEK THREE

Venus' sweet sextile with Mars blesses your love life with harmony and sensuality. This cosmic connection weaves an enchanting thread of passion and partnership, making it an ideal time to express your affection and desires to your beloved.

However, Mercury's opposition with the steadfast Saturn can cast a shadow on your communications. This celestial aspect may introduce challenges in expressing yourself, so it's crucial to choose your words carefully and be open to constructive criticism.

As Mercury gracefully enters diplomatic Libra, your conversational style takes on a more balanced and cooperative tone. You'll find it easier to navigate discussions and negotiations, fostering understanding and harmony in your interactions.

Nevertheless, Mercury's opposition with Neptune may bring a touch of confusion to your thoughts and conversations. It's essential to clarify misunderstandings and ensure you're on the same page with others.

SEPTEMBER WEEK THREE

🚀 Mercury's trine with both Uranus and Pluto ignites a spark of intellectual brilliance. Your mind becomes a powerhouse of innovative ideas, and you're equipped with the adaptability to welcome unconventional solutions.

❀ Venus' entry into practical Virgo grounds your approach to matters of the heart. You find pleasure in the details of your relationships, seeking to improve and perfect the art of love.

⚡ On the flip side, the square between Venus and Uranus introduces a dash of unpredictability into your love life. Expect unexpected turns and unconventional romantic interests that keep your heart on its toes.

☀ The Sun's opposition with responsible Saturn may present some challenges when asserting your authority and self-expression. To overcome these hurdles, use patience and a steadfast commitment to your goals.

🌑 The arrival of the New Moon marks a fresh start in your journey. It's the perfect moment to set new intentions and pursue self-discovery and personal growth with unwavering determination.

SEPTEMBER WEEK FOUR

💧 As Mars strides into Scorpio, your life takes on an intensity that's hard to ignore. Your desires deepen, your determination strengthens, and you're more than willing to go to great lengths to pursue your goals. This cosmic alignment ignites your passion and ambition. It's a time to tackle challenges head-on with fierce determination and unwavering focus. The energy of Mars in Scorpio urges you to confront the most profound aspects of your life and make transformative changes.

☉ The September Equinox, marking the shift of seasons, is a significant cosmic event. It's a reminder from the universe to seek balance in your life, much like the natural world adapts to changing seasons. Take stock of your goals, priorities, and the direction you're heading in. Find an equilibrium in the midst of change and transition.

♎ With the Sun's graceful entrance into Libra, your relationships take center stage. The cosmic spotlight shines on your interpersonal connections, encouraging you to seek harmony and fairness in all your interactions. You're naturally inclined to mend any imbalances, fostering a sense of equilibrium.

SEPTEMBER WEEK FOUR

⚡ The Sun's trines with Uranus and Pluto infuse your life with a potent blend of transformation and innovation. You become more receptive to change and open to new ideas and experiences.

☽ As the Moon moves into Scorpio, your emotional depths are summoned. You'll feel a profound urge to delve into your innermost feelings, motivations, and desires. It is a time for introspection, self-discovery, and understanding the driving forces behind your actions.

♨ However, the square between Mars and Pluto can intensify power struggles and conflicts. Approach such situations with tact, diplomacy, and a keen understanding of power dynamics. Avoid provoking unnecessary confrontations and instead seek common ground and cooperation.

⛰ The Moon's subsequent entry into Sagittarius brings a sense of adventure and expansion to your emotional landscape. Your feelings take on a more open and exploratory quality. You're drawn to new horizons, both in your intellectual pursuits and emotional experiences.

OCTOBER WEEK ONE

As the Moon graces Aquarius with its presence, a sense of liberation envelops you. The mundane takes a backseat, allowing your mind to embark on a journey of unconventional ideas and humanitarian causes. This lunar influence invites you to engage with your community and explore intellectual pursuits that might have seemed unusual before.

However, be aware of the cosmic tussle between Mercury and Jupiter in the form of a square. Your enthusiasm is commendable, but it could lead to a clash between the grand vision and the nitty-gritty details. To navigate this celestial puzzle, find a harmonious balance between optimism and the practicalities of projects.

Shifting into Pisces, the Moon invokes emotions reminiscent of a gentle, rolling sea. Empathy and compassion become your guiding stars. Now is an auspicious time for acts of kindness, as you're in tune with the needs of those around you. Creative and spiritual pursuits are your vessel for exploring your inner world. Embrace the flow of this celestial tide, weaving harmony in heart and mind.

OCTOBER WEEK ONE

🚀 With the Moon's transition to Aries, a surge of energy propels you into action. Your assertiveness and courage are magnified, allowing you to pursue your passions. This cosmic force inspires you to be proactive.

🕵 Meanwhile, Mercury's foray into Scorpio adds depth and intensity to your thinking. Your curiosity leads you to investigate matters with a keen eye, seeking the hidden truths. It's a period of profound introspection, where complex issues become captivating puzzles to unravel.

🌕 The Full Moon takes center stage, casting a radiant light on your path. This is the culmination, the moment of realization. Reflect upon the intentions you set during the New Moon and witness how they've blossomed. It's a cosmic juncture for letting go of what no longer serves you and stepping forward with newfound clarity.

🪨 However, a square between Mercury and Pluto adds a touch of intensity to your communication and thought processes. Your determination and focus are commendable, but guard against becoming fixated on ideas or entangled in power struggles.

OCTOBER WEEK TWO

☽ As the Moon gracefully saunters into Taurus, the cosmic energies gently guide you towards a more grounded and tactile experience. This lunar shift encourages you to revel in the beauty of the tangible world, to savor the touch of textures, and to find solace in the simplicity of life's pleasures. Your emotions take on a serene hue, urging you to appreciate the sensory richness that surrounds you.

✺ In the harmonious sextile between Venus and expansive Jupiter, the cosmic stage is set for a symphony of warmth and generosity in your relationships. This celestial alignment enhances the bonds you share, infusing them with a sense of abundance and goodwill. It's a time to indulge in shared pleasures and cultivate a spirit of generosity towards others.

♊ As the Moon transitions into communicative Gemini, your mental landscape becomes a fertile ground for exploration and curiosity. Ideas flow effortlessly, and there's a desire for engaging conversations that stimulate the intellect. It's a cosmic invitation to express your thoughts, connect with others, and revel in the free flow of ideas.

OCTOBER WEEK TWO

💜 Venus, now in Libra, adds a touch of elegance and charm to your interactions. However, an opposition with dreamy Neptune introduces a note of ambiguity. It's a reminder to navigate matters of the heart with clarity and discernment, avoiding idealizations.

🔄 Pluto's direct motion signals a profound cosmic shift, urging you to embrace transformative energies. This period encourages inner growth and the release of anything that hinders your evolution. It's a time to let go and welcome the transformative currents of change.

☀ The Moon's entrance into Leo infuses the atmosphere with a radiant and theatrical flair. Now is the time to express your authentic self, to bask in the spotlight of creativity, and to embrace a sense of self-assurance.

🌙 Venus, in a harmonious trine with innovative Uranus, invites a sprinkle of excitement into your love life and creative endeavors. This cosmic alignment encourages you to embrace spontaneity and be open to unconventional expressions of affection.

🌾 Venus's trine with Pluto deepens the emotional tapestry. This celestial dance invites transformation.

OCTOBER WEEK THREE

🌙 As the Moon gracefully transitions into Virgo, the cosmic spotlight shifts toward meticulous details and practical pursuits. This lunar phase encourages you to embrace a systematic approach to your tasks, finding satisfaction in the precision of your efforts. Attend to the finer points of life, channeling the Virgo energy to refine your routines and enhance your efficiency.

☀ The square between the radiant Sun and expansive Jupiter sparks a cosmic tension, urging you to find a balance between optimism and practicality. While Jupiter encourages you to dream big, the Sun in Virgo emphasizes the importance of grounded, realistic actions. It's a celestial call to temper your enthusiasm with a dose of pragmatism, ensuring that your aspirations align with steps toward achievement.

🌙 Transitioning into Libra, the Moon invites you into a harmonious space where balance and beauty become paramount. Libra's influence encourages you to seek harmony in your relationships and surroundings. Embrace the art of compromise and diplomacy, allowing the Libra Moon to guide you toward cooperation.

OCTOBER WEEK THREE

☿ Mercury's conjunction with assertive Mars amplifies your communication style, infusing it with vigor and determination. This celestial pairing empowers you to express your ideas with confidence, but be mindful of potential conflicts that may arise from passionate debates. Channel this energy into constructive dialogue and assertive decision-making.

● The New Moon marks a potent moment for new beginnings. Try setting intentions aligned with the Libra themes of balance, harmony, and relational growth. This lunar phase offers a cosmic canvas for planting seeds of intention that will blossom over the coming weeks. Reflect on your aspirations, particularly those related to partnerships and artistic endeavors, as you embark on a fresh lunar cycle.

☾ Entering Scorpio's mysterious realms, the Moon beckons you to explore the depths of your emotions and desires. This introspective phase encourages you to embrace transformation and release any emotional baggage. Dive into the profound currents of Scorpio's energy, allowing it to facilitate personal growth and renewal. ♏ ✦

OCTOBER WEEK FOUR

☾ Neptune's ethereal energy takes center stage as it gracefully ingresses Pisces, creating a dreamy and intuitive atmosphere. You may find your imagination heightened and your connection to the spiritual realms deepening. Allow the gentle waves of inspiration to guide your creativity and enhance your sense of compassion.

☼ As the radiant Sun ventures into Scorpio, the cosmic spotlight shifts towards matters of transformation and depth. This solar transit encourages you to explore the hidden facets of your life, fostering a sense of resilience and empowerment. Dive into self-discovery and embrace the potential for rebirth.

● The square between the Sun and Pluto adds an intense dynamic to the cosmic tapestry. This celestial dance prompts you to confront power dynamics and transformations within yourself and your relationships. Be prepared for a journey of self-reflection and a willingness to release what no longer serves your higher purpose.

OCTOBER WEEK FOUR

☿ Mercury continues its celestial journey, moving into Sagittarius. This shift infuses your mental landscape with a sense of adventure and a thirst for knowledge. Embrace the spirit of exploration and be open to expansive ideas that broaden your understanding.

♂ Mars' trine with Saturn brings a harmonious blend of assertiveness and discipline. This cosmic collaboration empowers you to pursue your goals with strategic precision. It's a time for focused effort and systematic progress, allowing you to build a solid foundation for your endeavors.

☿ However, Mercury's opposition to Uranus introduces an element of unpredictability to your thoughts and communication. Be open to unexpected insights and innovative ideas, but also be mindful of potential disruptions. Flexibility and adaptability are essential during this cosmic conversation.

♂ The sextile between Mercury and Pluto adds depth to your mental processes. This aspect encourages profound insights and transformative thoughts.

NOVEMBER WEEK ONE

♎ Venus squares Jupiter, creating a cosmic tension between the planet of love and beauty and the planet of expansion and abundance. This alignment may bring a conflict between indulgence and moderation, prompting you to find a balance between pleasure and responsibility in your relationships and desires.

🚀 Mars forms a harmonious trine with Neptune, blending the assertive energy of Mars with the dreamy and imaginative influence of Neptune. This cosmic collaboration encourages you to channel your actions toward creative and spiritually inspired pursuits. It's a time when your efforts are infused with inspiration and compassion.

♐ Mars makes its fiery entrance into Sagittarius, intensifying the adventurous and optimistic energies of this fire sign. Your actions are guided by a sense of exploration and a desire for new experiences. This transit encourages you to pursue your goals with a spirit of enthusiasm and a willingness to take risks.

🌳 As the Moon moves into Taurus, the cosmic energy shifts toward a more grounded and sensual atmosphere.

NOVEMBER WEEK ONE

⚡ Mars opposes Uranus, creating a dynamic and potentially disruptive influence. This cosmic combination may bring unexpected events, sudden changes, or a desire for freedom and independence. Exercise caution in your actions, and be open to adapting to unforeseen circumstances.

🌕 The Full Moon graces the sky, illuminating the cosmic landscape with its radiant glow. It is a culmination and a time of heightened emotions. Reflect on your achievements, release what no longer serves you, and embrace the transformative energy of the lunar cycle.

🌑 Mars sextile Pluto adds depth and intensity to your actions. There's a potent force driving your pursuits, allowing you to tap into your inner power and make significant progress. It's a time for strategic actions and positive transformations.

♀ Venus makes its entrance into Scorpio, intensifying the depths of passion and intimacy in your relationships. This transit invites you to explore the mysteries of love, delve into emotional connections, and embrace transformation in matters of the heart.

NOVEMBER WEEK TWO

🌀 Get ready for a profound cosmic shift as the electrifying planet Uranus makes its grand entrance into the steady realms of Taurus. This celestial event promises a period of radical transformation, urging you to embrace innovation and groundbreaking ideas, especially in the areas of stability and security. The cosmos is set for a dance of change, encouraging flexibility and an openness to new paradigms that could reshape your understanding of these foundational aspects of life.

💔 Venus square Pluto intensifies the cosmic drama, delving deep into the intricate dynamics of your relationships. This potent alignment prompts a powerful exploration of the shadows, urging you to confront and overcome challenges that may have been lingering beneath the surface. It's an astrological call to transform, evolve, and experience a profound rebirth.

🔄 Mercury, the planet of communication and thought, embarks on its retrograde journey, prompting a cosmic pause for introspection and review. This period encourages you to revisit old projects, relationships, and unresolved matters for resolution.

NOVEMBER WEEK TWO

🐻 The lunar spotlight then shifts to Leo, infusing the cosmic scene with creativity and self-expression.

🔍 Jupiter, the expansive planet, takes a reflective pause as it turns retrograde. This cosmic realignment invites you to reassess your personal beliefs, philosophies, and growth goals. Use this period as an opportunity for inner exploration, refining your path, and aligning your journey with your evolving aspirations.

🪨 Mercury's conjunction with Mars adds an assertive energy to communication and mental pursuits. Leverage this dynamic duo to express your thoughts assertively and tackle tasks with precision. However, be mindful of potential conflicts that may arise from impulsive words and actions.

🌾 The Moon's entrance into Virgo adds a practical and detail-oriented influence to the cosmic mix. This phase encourages you to focus on organization, efficiency, and meticulous attention to the finer points in your daily tasks. It's an excellent time for practical problem-solving and taking a discerning approach to your responsibilities.

NOVEMBER WEEK THREE

☼ The harmonious trine between the Sun and Jupiter illuminates your path with optimism and expansion. It's as if the universe is whispering encouragement, nudging you to explore new horizons and embrace the abundance that life has to offer.

☼ Sun's trine with Saturn brings a sense of structure and stability to your endeavors. Your efforts are rewarded, and you find that discipline and perseverance pave the way for long-lasting success. This cosmic alignment encourages you to build on solid foundations.

☿ Mercury, the planet of communication, engages in a dynamic sextile with transformative Pluto. Your thoughts and words carry a profound impact, and this cosmic alliance empowers you to delve into deep, meaningful conversations that foster growth and understanding.

♃ Mercury opposes Uranus, sparking a surge of unconventional ideas and unexpected twists in your thought processes. Be open to innovation and sudden flashes of insight as the cosmos encourages you to break free from mental constraints.

NOVEMBER WEEK THREE

● The New Moon marks a potent moment for fresh beginnings. It's a cosmic reset button, inviting you to set new intentions and sow the seeds for future growth. Take this opportunity to align your aspirations with the cosmic rhythms.

◯ The Sun's conjunction with Mercury intensifies the solar energy, enhancing your communication skills and mental clarity. Your mind is sharp, and you find it easier to articulate your thoughts and ideas.

♐ Mercury's shift into Sagittarius expands your mental horizons, infusing your thoughts with a sense of adventure and a thirst for knowledge. It's a time to explore new perspectives and embrace the broader tapestry of ideas.

♅ Uranus's sextile with Neptune introduces an electrifying yet harmonious energy. It's as if innovation and inspiration dance together, urging you to bring a touch of magic into your endeavors. Embrace the unexpected with an open heart.

⚡ The Sun's opposition to Uranus brings an element of surprise and unpredictability.

NOVEMBER WEEK FOUR

⊕ Communication gains a touch of grounded wisdom as Mercury forms a harmonious trine with Saturn. Your thoughts and words are infused with practicality and a long-term perspective.

✦ A celestial conversation between Mercury and Jupiter enhances your mental prowess and expands your intellectual horizons.

♇ The Sun forms a harmonious sextile with Pluto, infusing your journey with transformative energy. This celestial aspect empowers you to tap into your inner strength and make positive changes in your life. You have the resilience to overcome challenges and the power to influence your circumstances. Embrace this cosmic support to delve into personal growth and embrace the potential for positive transformation.

💬 The merger of Mercury and Venus brings a touch of charm and eloquence to your communication style. This cosmic alliance enhances your ability to express love, beauty, and harmony. It's a favorable time for heartfelt conversations, artistic pursuits, and connecting with others on a more harmonious level.

NOVEMBER WEEK FOUR

The cosmic harmony between Venus and Saturn brings stability and commitment to your relationships and creative endeavors. This alignment emphasizes the importance of building lasting foundations in matters of the heart and artistic pursuits. Your connections deepen, and your creative projects gain structure and longevity under this celestial influence.

Saturn, the cosmic taskmaster, resumes its forward motion, signaling a shift in the cosmic energies. As Saturn turns direct, you may feel a sense of progress in areas where you've been diligently working towards your goals. This celestial event encourages a disciplined and steady approach to your ambitions, helping you move forward with greater clarity and purpose.

The cosmic messenger, Mercury, resumes its direct motion, lifting the fog of retrograde energies. Communication flows more smoothly, and any delays or misunderstandings begin to resolve. Use this time to move forward with plans, make decisions, and express your thoughts with increased clarity.

DECEMBER WEEK ONE

☽ As the Moon gracefully enters Taurus, the cosmic stage is set for a harmonious dance of emotions. Sensuality and stability take the spotlight as Taurus' grounded energy embraces the lunar landscape. This period invites reflection on comfort, security, and the pleasures of life. Emotions find solace in the tangible and the familiar, guiding one to seek stability and indulge in earthly delights under the Taurus Moon's nurturing influence.

💗 Venus gracefully forms a sextile with Pluto, weaving an enchanting tale of transformation in matters of love and desire. This celestial alignment adds depth and intensity to relationships. The cosmic dance encourages a profound exploration of emotional connections, fostering a magnetic allure that captivates hearts and sparks a transformative journey in the realm of passion.

☽ The Moon gracefully transitions into Gemini, ushering in the energy of curiosity. Under the influence of the versatile Gemini Moon, emotions become mercurial, and the desire for stimulation takes center stage.

DECEMBER WEEK ONE

🌕 The cosmic spectacle unfolds with the arrival of the Full Moon, casting its luminous glow upon the celestial canvas. Emotions reach their peak as the Sun opposes the Moon in a cosmic ballet of light and shadow. It's a time of culmination, realization, and heightened sensitivity. Under the Full Moon's radiant beams, emotions come to fruition, and clarity is sought amid the cosmic glow.

🌙 Transitioning into Cancer, the Moon brings forth a nurturing and intuitive energy. Emotions swell like the tides, and a deep connection to home, family, and security becomes paramount. Cancer's watery embrace encourages a retreat into the sanctuary of emotions, inviting a time of self-care under the lunar influence.

☾ Mercury forms a harmonious trine with Neptune, creating a celestial harmony that weaves dreams into the fabric of communication. Under this ethereal alliance, words become poetic, and intuition guides the flow of thoughts. It's a time for imaginative expression, spiritual insights, and a deeper understanding of the mystical realms. Mercury and Neptune join forces, inviting a dance of creativity and intuition.

DECEMBER WEEK TWO

🚀 Mars squares off against the stoic Saturn, creating a cosmic tension that echoes the struggle between pushing forward and exercising patience. This celestial configuration prompts a thoughtful consideration of your actions. How can you assert yourself without stepping on others' toes? Find a balance between your desires and the practical limitations of the moment.

🔮 Neptune, the dreamy planet, pivots directly, lifting the cosmic veil that shrouded your dreams and aspirations. With newfound clarity, your inner visions and creative pursuits are revitalized. It's time to trust your instincts and set sail toward the ethereal realms of inspiration.

⚡ Mercury engages in a celestial tango with both Uranus and Neptune. The opposition with Uranus sparks innovative thoughts, breaking through mental barriers. Meanwhile, the trine with Neptune infuses your communication with empathy and imagination. As Mercury steps into Sagittarius, the realm of expansive ideas, let your thoughts roam freely and embrace a more adventurous mindset.

DECEMBER WEEK TWO

♎ The Moon's graceful ingress into Libra adds a touch of diplomacy to your emotional landscape. Relationships take center stage, and you're drawn to harmonize and find equilibrium in your interactions. It's a time to appreciate beauty, both in the world around you and within your connections. Focus on fairness in your relationships, and understand the beauty of equilibrium. Seek compromise and find the middle ground in emotional matters.

☿ Mercury's harmonious sextile with Pluto deepens the intellectual currents. Engage in meaningful conversations that have the power to transform. Your words carry a profound weight, so use them wisely to foster understanding and growth. Explore profound ideas and connect on a soulful level.

♂ Mars squares off against Neptune, creating a challenge between your desires and the elusive nature of dreams. Proceed with caution in your pursuits, ensuring that your actions are grounded in reality even as you reach for the stars. Navigate the waters of ambition with care, ensuring your dreams don't dissipate in the mist.

DECEMBER WEEK THREE

☽ The Moon, a master of emotional depth, slips into mysterious Scorpio, casting shadows that reveal the hidden corners of your soul. Embrace the intensity, for in the depths, you'll find the keys to emotional transformation.

♐ As the red warrior Mars dons the pragmatic robes of Capricorn, ambition and discipline become your cosmic companions. Your actions now carry the weight of purpose, and your strategic maneuvers propel you toward your goals.

☉ A cosmic showdown unfolds as the Sun squares off against stern Saturn. This celestial clash tests your resolve, demanding that you confront challenges with unwavering determination. In this cosmic crucible, your character is forged and strengthened.

● The New Moon graces the cosmic stage, marking the beginning of a lunar cycle. Set your intentions with clarity and focus, for the seeds you plant now will blossom in the coming weeks. It's a time of fresh starts and new beginnings.

DECEMBER WEEK THREE

🌑 The enigmatic Black Moon enters Sagittarius, casting shadows that prompt introspection. Dive into the hidden realms of your psyche, uncovering the wisdom that resides in the depths of your being.

○ Saturn's stern gaze meets the elusive Neptune in a cosmic square. Reality and dreams collide, urging you to find the delicate balance between the practical and the visionary. Ground your aspirations in the real world while maintaining a touch of magic.

💔 Venus, the planet of love, clashes with Saturn's stern energy, creating a celestial challenge in matters of the heart. It's a time to reassess relationships and commitments, ensuring they align with your long-term goals.

☀ The December Solstice marks the turning point, where the Sun's journey pauses before reversing course. It's a symbolic moment of reflection and renewal, inviting you to align with the rhythms of the cosmos.

♑ The Sun steps into the grounded realm of Capricorn, marking the beginning of a new astrological season. Practicality, ambition, and resilience become prominent.

DECEMBER WEEK FOUR

💜 As Venus engages in a celestial dance with Neptune, a beautiful yet potentially intricate energy surrounds matters of the heart. The lines between reality and fantasy might blur, emphasizing the importance of careful discernment in how you approach relationships. It's advised to be wary of overly idealizing situations or individuals and to strive for clarity in your emotional connections.

✦ Venus gracefully moves into the structured realm of Capricorn, bringing a sense of order and responsibility to your expressions of love and admiration for beauty. During this phase, practical considerations may influence your romantic endeavors, encouraging you to build strong foundations. Thoughtful gestures of love can be particularly impactful during this period.

☾ The Moon glides into the dreamy waters of Pisces, inviting you to explore the poetic landscapes of emotion and intuition. This celestial alignment heightens your sensitivity and compassion, providing an ideal moment for creative pursuits, meditation, or introspective journeys to connect with your inner self.

DECEMBER WEEK FOUR

☽ Experience a transformative shift in lunar energies as the Moon steps into the assertive realm of Aries. Feel the surge of initiative and a strong desire for action propelling you forward. Seize this dynamic force to confront challenges head-on and assert your individuality across various aspects of your life.

♣ Embark on a celestial journey as the Moon transitions into the grounded realms of Taurus. Immerse yourself in the pleasures of the material world, savoring and finding solace in the stability of your surroundings. Embrace the tactile and sensory experiences that this lunar phase offers.

☐ Witness a celestial tussle as Mercury engages in a cosmic dance with Saturn, creating tension between communication and structure. This alignment calls for thoughtful and deliberate expression, urging you to navigate potential challenges or limitations in conveying your ideas. Exercise patience and diligence in your communication efforts, utilizing this time to refine your thoughts and concepts.

NOTES

NOTES

NOTES

Astrology, Tarot & Horoscope Books.

Mystic Cat

www.ingramcontent.com/pod-product-compliance
Lightning Source LLC
LaVergne TN
LVHW051844080426
835512LV00018B/3059